FLYING EACH
OTHER HOME

CORVID PRESS

FIRST EDITION

ISBN 979-8-9921117-0-5

Website: sjlynne.com
Instagram: @sj_lynne

Cover design by Andrew Kinsey
www.kinseydesign.com

FLYING EACH OTHER HOME

poems by
S.J. Lynne

Contents

Far From Home

The Way Back Home

Arriving Home

To all the crows who flew me home
when I could not see the way.

FAR FROM HOME

THE PERFECTIONIST

I'll keep apologizing
until I stop blundering my words.

I'll keep searching
until I find someone who can answer my impossible
questions.

I'll keep watching others
until I've learned what not to do.

I'll keep finding out
how not to live.

I'll keep silent
until I have just the right words to say.

I'll keep watching my heroes fail
until I fail as a hero and know how it feels.

I'll keep striving for perfection
until I get home.

ONCE UPON A TIME

Once upon a time,
a polar bear came from the south
and asked the daughter of Eve
if she would dance.
And the dancing bear
carried her away on painted wings.
The rains came,
and the wings melted
and left the fur matted.
The wind came
and chilled the girl.
The sleet came
and froze their feet.
The sun came
and thawed them both,
and dried them both,
and burned them both,
and blazed on
brighter than before the storm,
and kept them warm.
And they danced away,
East of the Sun
and West of the Moon,
to the sound of the North
and the music of the stars.

THE DANCERS

Who is that girl in the mask?
Who is that man with the beard?
He thought she was beautiful.
She thought he was weird.

Yet here they dance together.
No one could tear them apart.
For when she holds his hand,
He surely holds her heart.

SONNET I

If thought the norm are Disney princess eyes,
Then his green orbs outsize them all with ease.
Coke bottle glasses shrink them down in size,
And even more so does the dragon's sneeze.
Those feckless freckles fracture flawless white.
His callouses from countless pages turned,
And knees that creak with old man's stiffened blight.
His hide he hides from sun, lest it be burned.
With stride oft lithe, not blithe, and measured haste
He hurries home to isolation sweet.
His time and energies he hates to waste
On tiresome tasks and needlessly moved feet.
    Yet this old man in young man's frame I think
    Is just the sort of fellow worth my ink.

SONNET II

I keep your love in boxes, cardboard hearts
Containing countless letters of your ink.
Your words fly to me from a land apart
And give me buoyant thoughts on days I sink.
Despite the distance, passion never slacks.
Reminders of your love to steady me
You send in envelopes and piled stacks,
As numerous as leaves upon a tree.
Oh, how does paper carry so much weight?
So light a thing to give my spirit wings
Yet anchor my soul and to help me wait
Until we meet again and my heart sings.
    Send love to me again, and it will keep
    In cardboard boxes while apart we sleep.

SONNET III

This bench was made for sitting. Let her sit.
She will not budge for this man's pleasure, she.
She turns now taciturn and, quitting wit,
Contents herself to wait for him to flee.
Yet neither leaves the metal cold and black,
Though come the rain and snow and sun and sleet.
The wind comes now to blow the grey clouds back,
Three hours passed from when they first did meet.
Five minutes and no more was what he said,
Though she protested all his needless haste,
And soon three years was the time that was sped.
Now not a second more the lovers waste.
    So may the bench endure as evidence
    Three score years more weath'ring the elements.

SONNET IV

You try to cheer me with your puns and wit
When I feel down, but oft I'd like to be
Alone with my own thoughts. So would you quit?
You spin my head in circles. Can't you see
That I can't figure out how your thoughts wend?
You reference science, politics, and more
Than my slim scope can ever comprehend.
Sometimes you even mention foreign lore,
And all allusions lost on me just leave
Me more confused than any should condone.
My husband, oh, why can you not conceive
Your jokes are better left for you alone?
    But since you can't contain yourself, you've won.
    If word play be the food of love, play on.

SONNET V

These polar bears are creatures of the cold.
They hate the heat and sun and warmer clime.
And yet his homeland, so I may be told,
Is getting warmer nearly all the time.
His whitish fur protects him from the chill.
What need has he of extra coverings?
I'm sure he'd like to shed some hairs and still
Have more than his fair share of cozy things.
The snow and ice befit him best, it's true.
The flakes of white—his dearest friends to see.
Yet cold he barely gets the whole year through
Since moving south to be with his love—me.
    At piles of blankets he will simply scoff
    Then beg of me, "Please turn the heating off."

BE GOOD

When I was just a little girl
 My father'd say, "Be good,"
Each time he'd tuck me in at night.
 And it was understood

That by turning out the bedroom light
 And then turning his back,
I would not get up for a drink
 Or bother him for a snack.

Yet looking back on it, I think
 I must have got it wrong.
Even though he was cleverly
 Imprinting all along.

His words "be good" still severely
 Ring in my head like an alarm
Anytime I think that I
 Might cause another harm.

But hard as I would often try,
 Harm still would come my way.
What should I have expected
 When every single day

Of my childhood recollected
 Includes the mem'ry of
Walking on eggshells 'round someone
 Who taught me, "This is love"?

It's loving for tempers to come undone
    When I break a single order,
Even the ones he hadn't shared
    With his perfectionistic daughter.

Because if I had really cared,
    I would have read his mind.
Predicting each and every whim
    Was the best way to be kind.

And so I learned my best from him
    How one was to "be good"
And kind and loving and all the things
    A godly woman should.

So when my way the Good Lord brings
    A potential lifetime partner
I do exactly as I'd been told.
    Therefore it shouldn't be a wonder

That in winter the house was always cold,
    And eggshells covered the floors,
And I was often left alone
    Behind closed bedroom doors,

And I was expected to atone
    For things I'd done as tasked,
Because I hadn't gone above
    What he'd actually asked.

Because it isn't really love
    Unless your own dreams are dead
And "good is never good enough"
    Fills your sleeping mind instead.

WONDERFUL

I can't remember when
The name you picked for me,
The one you had engraved
Inside your ring,
Started to mean

    Woefully unintelligent,

    Overly burdensome,

    Not to be trusted,

    Devoid of desirability,

    Emotionally unstable,

    Requiring supervision,

    Freeloading, flaky,

    Unoriginal, uninspiring,

    Lacking ambition.

But I think it happened slowly,
Until the word, a weal unhealed,
Made my eardrums deaf to praise—
Rendered senseless to the sound
Of Wonderful.

THE FIRST THING YOU EAT IS YOUR TONGUE

When Love leaves you hungry,
the first thing you eat to survive is your tongue.
Not all at once, no.
One
tiny
piece
at a time.
It's convenient, easily hidden.
Just keep your mouth shut.
    Don't make a sound.

He wasn't listening anyways
to your cries of,
Please, sir. I want some more.
    Don't you know how much it costs to feed you?
    You should be grateful.

Vocal chords are next,
strung out like spaghetti,
choked down.
    Don't make a sound.

Teeth are last—
crunchy
little
delicacies.
No bark, no bite—
no flavor.
Sustenance un-sustaining.

Would it even matter now
if someone rescued you,
came along and fed you,
if you can no longer swallow,
                speak, or chew?

AFTER THE FIRST THREE MONTHS, THE NEXT THREE YEARS—IN THREE LINES

You didn't break it.
Still refused to do the wash.
I fold all your shirts.

> Tone condescending,
> Just like talking to a cat.
> I'm a thing you own.

"So intelligent!"
Question ev'ry decision.
Can I trust myself?

> "Squishy squishy squish
> Squishy squishy squishy squish—"
> Please don't call me that.

"There's so much of you.
I want to touch all of you.
That's stomach, or boob?"

> "I'm sorry that I
> Keep hurting you. Guess I'm just
> good at it. Don't leave."

"Do not talk to me."
I leave you alone and cry.
"Don't know why you're mad."

> Shoes worn through the sole.
> I searched for hours, bought you new.
> Refused the new shoes.

Tape on all the floors.
"Step around those spots. They creak."
I pulled up the tape.

FIXER UPPER

I used to write you sonnets—praised your frame,
Your sightless eyes, your freckles. And I should
Have written thousands more if not your wood
Had rotted out, o'erused behind closed doors.
But now the house is full of sagging floors
That creak in ways I find distasteful. Still,
I'd rehabilitate you, cure your ills,
Could I but find the scourge's hidden source.
With all my art and tools I could not force
The reason why your heart stopped pumping blood
Below your waist, and all it did was flood
Your cheeks with scarlet sigils of your shame.
    For though I know you tried with all your might
    You couldn't get yourself to stay upright.

THE LAST DAY

Arms encircling,
But refusing to touch me.
Semblance of embrace.

                              Your search history.
                    There were so many of them.
                       Breathing comes in gasps.

Anger replaces shock.
Rip off your shirt I'm wearing.
I pick up the phone.

                              I lift up my eyes.
                    Help comes from my mom and friends.
                       The packing begins.

I leave garlic salt,
Seven boxes of letters,
And both of my rings.

                              It's not happening,
                    Not to me. I'm just watching
                       Someone else's life.

Come home, confront you.
Eyes cast down, YOU ask for hugs?
I'm kinder than you.

                              Rain drops start falling.
                    Windshield wipers are useless.
                       Storm breaks overhead.

BROKEN BENCH

What do I say the day "forever" ends,
When once I promised that I'd stay for life?
No longer lovers, confidants, or friends.
Mistrust has severed husband from his wife.
I said I'd weather every storm, but this—
This one shakes all foundations once secure.
The thunder rolls. The lightning won't desist.
A few drops here and there—it starts to pour.
The wind whips up a frenzy, blowing rain
Across my field of vision. Benches break,
All tossed about by tempests. Shattered panes
Of glass come clatt'ring down around. I make
    A run for safer hills through mud and mire.
    I catch my breath, and see the sky catch fire.

THE WORST THAT COULD BE SAID OF HER

drinking [ˈdɹɪŋk●ɪŋ]
adj.
consuming two or fewer alcoholic beverages a month
"A drinking woman has substantial moral issues."

tatted [ˈtætɪd]
adj.
proudly sporting her first meaningful tattoo
"Being tatted makes her look like the rest of the world."

fashion designer [ˈfæʃən dɪˈzaɪnɚ]
n.
a person who designs and builds costumes for a local non-profit Christian theatre company
"She switched her career from teaching, something familiar and purposeful, and decided to become a fashion designer instead."

LATER

Didn't give you time?
You had seven years to change.
Weren't you listening?

> Emails pierce inbox.
> You fire shots from a distance.
> "Needn't read." I do.

"Not a psychopath."
So the self-assessment lied?
Lying to yourself.

> You quit therapy
> When you realized that it
> Wouldn't bring me back.

You said you'd take me
Back, but also you wish that
I had died, not left.

> Lockdown starts that spring.
> I thank God I'm not with you
> For March Madness.

"When our parents are dead,
I won't talk to her again."
You called her, lonely.

> Moved to Iowa.
> Tried to get away from me.
> Found some peace at last.

BACKTRACKING

I was so (stupid) proud
that I planned our wedding for
less than three thousand dollars.

I wore my grandma's dress, and
you wore your father's suit.
I made your vest. We
got married in a tiny chapel and
had a reception at the park.
Your dad
fixed the fuse box
in the pavilion, and I
scrubbed the bathrooms,
scared the spiders out, like
Cinderella before the ball.
    Made the decorations.
    Made the dessert.
    Made the decision.

So how surreal it was
to realize
our divorce would cost just
a third of that.
    Say the words.
    Serve the papers.
    Sign the name.

The notary at the DMV
makes the stamp and says,

"Next."
    A casualty.
    Another day at the office.
    A marriage happening in reverse.

I wonder what is "next,"
as I start to backtrack
through the last four years
to find the fork where I should have
turned and run the other way.

THE WAY BACK HOME

FLYING EACH OTHER HOME

I've heard it said that
People come into our lives for a reason
and
We're all just walking each other home
and
People are meant to go through this life two by two
and

for the kid who grew up with friends far and few
     between
even two felt like an abundance.
Three, a miracle.
More, an impossibility.
It's levi-O-sa.
And they'd scatter like birds.
But that's fine,
because a bird would never lead me home,
just farther *into the woods*
and leave me *halfway through*
to find my own way back.
A blue bird did that once,
enticed me deep into the brambles, promising berries,
but he'd already eaten them all,
and like an unseelie creature
lured me into lostness.
Levio-SA.
The spell was broken,
and I could not rise up to heights above the branches
where the sun's rays might have shown me the way out.

I said to my soul, be still and wait without hope,
because they tell you that when you're lost
the best thing you can do is stay put.
So I sat in the dark,
and by and by the coven came—
a chorus of crows to comfort me.
One, a woman acquainted with sorrows.
Two, a dreamer of more joyful tomorrows.
Three, a sister.
Four, a listener.
Five, with silver needles laden.
Six, Summer's golden maiden.
Seven, the secret I couldn't keep—
and more I couldn't count.
All to lead me through the forest deep.
Feathers black as night—
ill omen for the shadows creeping—
flying each other home.

REBECCA SUSAN

Four thousand years ago
We gathered roots and berries just outside the village,
Lamenting over the lads who wouldn't notice us
And *tsking* at the number of acorns on the forest floor,
　　foretelling the hard winter ahead.

Two thousand years ago
You held my hand while I miscarried, and you sang to
　　me, smoothed my hair.
You told me it would be alright,
Even though we both knew when I closed my eyes, I
　　wouldn't see you again in this lifetime.

One thousand years ago
Your roof caught fire on Beltane after your son decided
　　to take a friend up on a dare.
The cat escaped with eight of its lives,
And we stayed awake all night hauling buckets to put
　　out the flames.

Four hundred years ago
I nursed your youngest through a fever, but the others
　　called me a witch when their own children died.
I fled with my family on a boat to the new world,
And the tears we wept on the dock at our parting could
　　have filled the sea between us.

One hundred years ago
We lived side by side and shared a garden, made

blankets for our husbands in the war.
It was a Tuesday in April when you got a letter lined in
     black,
And I held you as we knelt in the front yard and watered
     the daffodils together.

Twenty-seven years ago
We shared animal crackers and apple juice in Sunday
     school.
I asked my parents if I could sit with you.
We didn't remember meeting before, but something
     tugged at us—a string unseen.

Twenty years ago
I fell into your lap as you sat in the front pew, wearing
     black—
Your brother and father laid out among the lilies.
Too traumatized for tears, your eyes were dry. So this
     time I cried for us both.

Eight years ago
We woke at dawn to sweep the spiders away and scrub
     the urinals,
Our fingers freezing.
I watched you disappear through the doors ahead of me,
     the last of my girlhood being swallowed up by the
     tireless trudge of time.

Two weeks ago
You walked to my house in the rain, and we drank gin
     and ate pizza

And watched Princess Diaries again.
We talked about our jobs and our dreams and our losses
and our loves as we drifted off to sleep on the couch.

And a hundred years from now,
And a thousand years from now,
And a hundred thousand years from now,
When the oceans have all dried up
And the stars have all gone out,
You will still be there
And so will I.

JENNY

We were instructed to walk, jog, and run.
And though we knew some of our classmates slept,
While others thought that sprinting was more fun,
A slow and steady pace was what we kept.
A jest of "walk, walk, walk" in uniform,
Made all the more ironic by the fact
That two souls such as ours would ne'er conform.
We've proven o'er the years that what we lacked
In speed has ten times over been repaid
By vistas, valleys, vaulting mountains seen
On roads not often traveled. Best plans laid
To rest, replaced by what has often been
    The less conventional path of the two.
    No one I'd rather walk it with than you.

MANDY

Little girls, we stewed twigs, earth, and berries,
Mixing up concoctions we called potions.
Made up spells, consorted with the fairies.
Parents scolded, called them evil notions.
We were taught to fear our inner magic.
Let them take our voices, left us silent,
Severed from ourselves. The wound was tragic.
Patched it with a love that soon turned violent.
In our darkest hours we recalled it—
Who we were before they lit our pyres.
What they tried to kill rose from the ash pit,
Purified by nights of hellish fires.
    Sisters, each a maiden, crone, and mother,
    Found at last pure love in one another.

BREAKFAST SONG

Guten Morgen, mein Katz.
Vie geht es ihnen?
Guten Morgen, klein Arschloch.
Vie geht es ihnen?
Guten Morgen, schwarz Leere.
Vie geht es ihnen?

EDREA

The prophecy was spoken ages hence
That barnyard fowl would one day overrun
The globe, impeded not by paltry fence.
The hens would have their own day in the sun.
Though signs were everywhere, they couldn't see
The rubber chickens coming home to roost.
Now feathered friends are roaming wild and free.
Mere anarchy upon the world is loosed.
They couldn't cage us in, though hard they tried
With pecking orders, principles, and more.
We flew the coop. They couldn't clip our wings.
Refused to be bruised, battered, and deep-fried.
    And now it's time to settle up the score.
    Our legacy will rival that of kings.

PILISA

A soft and supple cherry blossom pink,
With dark smooth bark of nine-and-twenty rings.
Articulative branches dripping ink,
Memorializing words her heartwood sings.
In growing towards the ever-shifting light
Her trunk twists 'round to find the brightest spot.
Deep roots delve down, defying death and blight,
And phototrophic foliage riots rot.
Let never axe cry "havoc!" 'gainst the grain.
Dismantling fruit and flower disavow.
Established in the orchard and unslain,
Her beauty praised forever, as 'tis now.
    A crown of roses for thy maiden's head!
    All talk of cherries cease! Get thee to bed.

POCKETS

If a pocket was a person
It would be you.
Always holding space,
Often filled up only to be emptied again,
Because your volume is precious and
Should be reserved for the most special things
Like tissues at weddings
And funerals
And exactly the right amount of change to pay for the
groceries
And the perfect skipping rock picked up on the shore but
saved for another time,
Or maybe for always.
Sometimes in need of mending,
Occasionally getting holes.
Take care of yourself,
Or ask someone else to take care of you for a change,
Because you are too important not to.
Always taken for granted.
Desired by women everywhere.
Conspicuous and sorely missed when you are absent.
I wish that I could shrink you down
And keep you in my pocket.
And when someone complimented my dress
I'd say, "Thanks! It has pockets."
And as proof, I'd pull you out of yourself
And show you off to the world.

ODE TO SALEM

A fireplace rimmed with dry stacked stone.
    Bedrooms aplenty, and bathrooms, too.
Yard enough to spare, though overgrown.
    She was a wish at last come true.
Of course the listing failed to mention
Dubious repairs made with frugal intention,
    But now it was mine to own.
And let us never forget the four species—
Cat, human, rabbit, and mouse—of feces
    I found in the first week alone.

Every single faucet leaked,
    Leaving trails of mold behind,
Rotten wood, and floors that squeaked.
    But how, O how, could I ever mind?
The air conditioning was full of mice,
And the baseboard heating was half as nice—
    Some thoughtless child, destruction had wreaked
With many a misplaced pill, penny, pen.
Piss puddles created the smell of a fen.
    Do not ask me to tell how the freezer reeked.

Cat vomit dotted every horizontal plane.
    Nicotine yellow covered every wall
And ceiling, leaving a permanent stain.
    Sticky residue absorbed all light, cast a pall.
As the curtains came down, sun wandered in
And danced in the dust. The rays were thin,
    Filtered through ginkgo leaf and crusted pane.

The roof at the back, I also found,
Was not entirely sealed or sound
    And let in the wet when it would rain.

With every carpet pulled back from the floor,
    Every piece of wallpaper peeled,
And every unhinged splintering door,
    Another travesty was revealed.
Four times my mother scrubbed the range,
And in the kitchen found something strange—
    She'd taken on the hardest chore.
As she scrubbed the sickly ceiling,
She found spaghetti that had been congealing
    And had hardened there years before.

The backyard had been littered with trash
    And termite-riddled rotting boards.
A firepit with melted plastic and ash
    Complemented the mosquito hordes
That I suspected annually spawned
From a koi-filled swamp that was once a pond—
    Now no more than an unsightly gash.
What had once been tenderly maintained—
Flower beds, lily pads—would have to be drained
    And evicted of amphibians who loved to splash.

You may very well ask—indeed, you should—
    Why I would purchase such a place
Filled with filth and molding wood—
    In short, an absolute disgrace.
I could handle being called "crazy"—

At least they'd never say I'm lazy—
    For buying the most fright'ning fixer upper I could.
But when they all called me "brave"
I felt my resolve cave.
    How could this ever be anything good?

Alone in my walls, disease all around,
    I started to paint, and polish, and shine.
I ripped up the weeds, put new plants in the ground.
    At least I had something I could finally call mine.
I got myself a small shadow that likes to shed,
And at night my familiar sleeps under my bed.
    And although my anxiety does still abound
When I look at the work that will never cease,
I remind myself why I named my house "peace"
    And choose to be grateful for the home that I've
    found.

FAITH

Two inches to the left of true desire
Is where I often find myself these days.
I cannot quite bring myself to aspire,
Sir, to become the object of your gaze.
I see you look my way with longing eyes,
Your gentle hands encircling my waist.
My disbelief, it mingles with surprise—
So sure was I my lips of poison taste.
Why else would my last lover spurn me so?
And surely once you've also had your fill,
You'll void your stomach, turn from me, and go.
But your physician's kiss bears no ill will.
    I sigh as much from pleasure as relief.
    Lord, help me overcome my unbelief.

JESSICA

I bought myself a single rose
    On that first Valentine's Day.
You'd never have gotten me one of those.
    "Too expensive," you would say.

Years ago, you said to me,
    "I'll never buy you flowers."
And as I stood there, shamefully,
    I felt your scowls and glowers.

They were not worth the cost, you said,
    Though you got me roses twice.
When you proposed and when we wed,
    You deemed them worth the price.

And as a miser hoards his gold,
    You were stingy with affection.
You thought my pleasure cheaply sold,
    I realized upon reflection.

But I am worth a kingdom's ransom!
    I shouted in my head.
Though I'd no suitors tall nor handsome,
    No one to share my bed,

No one to buy me a bouquet,
    Or share a cup of tea,
No one to wipe the tears away,
    I still had a lover—me.

All thoughts of you began dispelling,
    And with it went the shame.
I doubt there was a more sweet-smelling
    Rose of another name.

For there before me in the stall
    Of the crowded marketplace,
Pink Jessica, as she was called,
    Gazed up into my face.

I knew I couldn't let her rot.
    She was worth three bucks and more.
So picking the best one from the lot,
    I paid and left the store.

I took her home, gave her a drink,
    And placed her in a vase.
And though I don't much care for pink,
    A fairer rose there never was.

ODE TO ADDERALL

Brain releases dopamine in spurts,
    And I find it difficult to explain
How something like a bright light hurts
    Or sounds too loud cause pain.
Focus slips away, and memories fade.
      Impulse veers off course, steers the wheel,
        Distracted by every single side quest.
But focus sharpens like a blade,
    Boring jobs gain more appeal—
      A simple pill puts racing thoughts to rest.

Tiny capsule, marian in hue,
    Opens the mind, narrows thought,
Clears the clouds blocking out my view,
    Challenges the norms I once was taught.
Living life on hard mode all those years,
      Never knowing there was another setting.
        Now I play knowing I can win.
No longer plagued by deep-seated fears
    Or spending countless hours regretting
      Tasks I couldn't finish—or even begin.

Stimulants have got a rotten wrap
    From years of being over-prescribed.
And others who use them end up in a trap.
    They're not a silver bullet as described.
Never meant to be the sole solution.
      But with therapy and other things combined,
        I've learned how to let myself be kind

And provide the needed absolution
  For the years I struggled against my mind.
    At last, I find my inner world aligned.

EDEN

There's a garden in Cocalico,
    Derelict for many a year.
Poison berries and ivy grow
    Too thick for pruning shear.
The soil there has been defiled.
The weeds and willow trees grow wild
And invite the curious child
    Who dares to rush in here.

A guardian of trumpet vine
    With petals all aflame
Looms o'er the gate, once by design,
    Now rambling without shame,
Shrubs and flowers all-consuming;
Perennial flourishing unresuming
Due to discipline-refusing
    Verdant tentacles untame.

Yet pallid pinions flitter
    Underneath the barren bough.
Life in the leafy litter
    Scurries, slithers even now.
Though roots are buried deep,
I'm told they do but only sleep
Between the worms that creep,
    Awaiting spade and plow.

Vernal blossoms long forgotten
    Begin to spring anew.

What once was cursed and rotten
    Is now doused in rain and dew
And strengthened by the rays
Of the sun on length'ning days.
And a dappled dalliance plays
    On every bloom in view.

Not quite Eden—further East—
    This garden here once fallowed,
From the curse at last released
    By one baleful berry swallowed.
The child reached out her hand
To the ripe fruit of the land—
As impulsive and unplanned
    As the consequence that followed.

It wasn't everlasting death;
    She found in her mouth instead
The juice of Justice. Kin of Seth
    Took hold of the homestead.
Hers to tend, hers to tame,
Hers to honor, hers to name,
Hers to rid of spoil and shame—
    A field for sweat and bread.

She savors sweetness from the earth
    As reward for all her toil.
Reenacting her own rebirth,
    Made of mud and soil.
The honey comb is dripping
With every drop of sweetness slipping.

There's milk and cream for whipping,
 And glistening golden oil.

Her children Hunger will not know,
 Nor wandering alone,
Nor Winter's cold, nor sleet, nor snow.
 There's no sin to atone—
No one to keep outside the gates,
Wondering what trial awaits,
Designed by fickle gods or fates—
 Just reaping what's been sown.

BLUE DEVILS

I was passing by the game store,
    And I thought I saw you there.
I nearly caused an accident,
    So intently I did stare.

But it was just a little boy,
    Maybe only nine or ten.
Of course it couldn't have been you,
    I thought to myself. But then...

A few weeks later I find out
    You've been back four months or more.
So it could have well been you
    I saw outside that store.

I keep seeing devils everywhere,
    In that same shade of blue.
My heart starts pounding in my chest
    When I think it might be you.

All my muscles feel like lead,
    And my stomach starts to churn.
I swear I'll never understand
    Why you decided to return.

You hated it, you always said,
    This place that I called home.
Afraid that you would end up "stuck,"
    You decided that you'd roam.

But I guess out west they didn't have
    Whatever it was you wanted.
A few years later you came back.
    And you thought YOU felt haunted?

These incubi in azure hue
    My restless dreams still plague.
Nightmares where you show up again,
    Intentions anything but vague.

And if you were to ask me,
    I couldn't say which one is worse:
To dread for years a chance encounter,
    Or for you to orchestrate one first.

At least I have my crows to warn me.
    Their black feathers are my shield
For when blue devils come crawling
    Out of some distant soy bean field.

ARRIVING HOME

UNPACKING

Although I truly would like nothing more
Than to step 'cross the threshold and go in,
I know as soon as I walk through that door
The real work of unpacking will begin.
Arriving home should be a joyful act.
Put up your feet, relax. The journey's done.
But all your shit still needs to be unpacked—
Then laundry, sorting mail, a grocery run.
Preparing for reentry sparks new fears.
My body feels the pull, begins to shake.
Will I survive arrival? Slept for years—
And dreams disintegrate when I awake.
     The vision in my head, what home should be—
     Will it come crashing with reality?

I KEPT SOME OF YOUR STUFF

I kept some of your stuff—
Not the hoodies or the notes,
But the noticing of vanity license plates
And the words poaceae and lepidoptera
And Cassiopeia and Billy Joel.
I donated the food processor—
Because using it for smoothies gave me panic attacks,
And you always hated cleaning it,
Even though I never asked you to—
And I threw out complaining about traffic
And counting stoplights on the way home from work.
Ulysses S. Grant and Alexander the Great
Can both rot in hell.
I'm not sure what to do with dancing yet,
And the smell of Little Caesar's turns my stomach.
So does caraway.
But my spinach is huge,
And my garden is full of cats.
Wouldn't you be jealous?
I kept Moiraine and Mat, but not March Madness.
I kept Avril. She keeps me company when I vacuum the
    house you never wanted,
The house I now call "home."
I kept the color green
And calzones
And the hopefulness of wild berries just around the next
    corner of the hiking trail.
I kept skipping rocks and seasoning pasta sauce that
    came in a jar.

There are still some of your things I've been trying to get
    rid of,
Like anxiety at leaving an odd number of eggs in the
    carton,
Or apologizing for not sneezing silently,
Or acquiring things on sale or not at all.
But no one will buy them, and the garbage man won't
    take them.
So I shove them in a box and bury them under a shrub
    in the garden
And pray they'll decay and create compost
And feed the new things thriving there
That your hands have never refused to touch
And your eyes have never had the chance to disapprove
    of.
And all the things I kept I now display proudly on the
    wall
Next to Julian and Mary and Bridgette
And the painting I bought in Nigeria—
All the things you taught me to love
Next to the things you never let me teach you to love
And never understood.
And it is very good.

WHY DID I LEAVE?

It wasn't because I was in love with someone else.
(I was.)
It wasn't because I thought I'd be better off with
    someone else.
(I might have been.)
It wasn't because other women didn't leave.
(I could never make that choice for them.)
It wasn't to punish you.
(I don't think you needed my help with that.)

So why did I leave?

Tonight, I'm standing at the sink washing dishes.
(I'm weeping.)
Tonight, I try not to think about the debt piling up and
    the financial security I had with you.
(I'm not successful.)
Tonight, it's been almost four years.
(I'm still alone.)
Tonight, I pray again for a partner to hold me, to help
    me.
(I'm not sure anyone is listening.)

I left for this?

Tonight, I put on a dress that makes me feel beautiful,
    and I wear makeup.
(You do not tell me I look like a whore.)
Tonight, I laugh at my own jokes.

(You do not say I'm too loud, or not funny.)
Tonight, I don't feel like cooking and buy myself enough
    Chinese food for two people.
(You do not ask how much it costs, complain about the
    smell, or call me squishy.)
Tonight, I sing and dance in the kitchen.
(You do not belittle my taste in music.)

I left for this.

Tonight, I thank myself for leaving.
(I left for her.)
Tonight, I hold myself tight around the shoulders.
(I left for us.)
Tonight, I help myself to another slice of cheesecake.
(I left for me.)
Tonight, freedom rings from every leaky faucet and
    crooked cobweb corner.
(Praise God.)

OCEANS

I used to hate crying.
Face like a tomato,
snot mixing with tears.
Not cute.

When I was very little,
    couldn't get calm,
        slow my breathing,
            stop catastrophizing.
Asthma attacks from crying so hard.
And not being able to breathe—
on top of being
    angry,
        sad—
            scared
me.

So I think I learned to be
scared of crying,
much the same way I
was scared of doing anything
until I knew I could do it perfectly.

For the first time today I realized
just what a wonder tears are.
Our eyes,
which are windows to the soul,
    leak,
        dribble,

flood
oceans of emotion.

Can't keep the ocean behind glass,
foolish to try.
Throw open the sash,
pour it out—
    soul-spilling,
        soul-seething,
            soul-soothing.
What a wonder! What a gift.
A different chemical composition for every emotion.
The most potent painkillers known to mankind.

I want to find the first person who ever told me
not to cry and
    drip,
        drop,
            dive
through their windows,
plug up the drains,
turn all the faucets on.
See? This is good. You try.

I was born crying.
My body has never not known
how to cry perfectly,
to declare loudly that
    I feel,
        I need,
            I am—

tomato-faced, snot-nosed,
over-flowing ocean.

SECOND WIFE

Remember well the way you used to jest,
"Now, if you think my wife is passing fair,
Just wait until you all behold the next."
As if you'd find another to compare!
Come, let us, you and I, argue it out.
Does she have ruddy rays to grace her head?
Or does she have the same wild way about
Her, stops your thoughts and pulls you to her bed?
How wide the river running 'twixt her thighs?
Do her hips wend like ways among the hills?
How patient is she with your moods and sighs?
And have you found my match in wits and wills?
　　Too late you learned that God made only one.
　　You never know a good thing till it's gone.

FORGIVENESS

You say I am repeating
something I have said before. I shall say it again
and again
and again.
Until it loses all meaning
and finds it again.

I have forgiven you so many times,
for so many things.
Seventy times seven
times seven
times seven.
>   *I'm sorry I keep hurting you,*
>   *I guess I'm just good at it.*
And you were
so good
so good.
>   *Be good.*

But the thing I haven't forgiven you for yet
is all of the time you took
convincing me you loved me,
and the time I spent believing you.
Maybe one day when I forgive myself of that,
I will finally be able to say
with my whole chest,
>   *I forgive you.*

For now, all I can say is this—

That I hope you are only ever
as miserable as you choose to be,
and that you find healing
and a separate peace,
as I am
slowly
finding mine.

THE POWER OF A NAME

In fantasy it is a well-known trope
That names contain enormous stores of pow'r.
So why'd I waste a single living hour
Called aught but my own given name, Miss S—?
Perhaps it was because I wanted to
Belong to someone else, avoid the shame
Of being lonely. So I took your name—
Or so I thought. Now mine belonged to you.
I gave up half myself, all for your pride.
The quest took years to find her, bring her home.
In search of her, I journeyed far and wide
And found at last her title in a tome.
    T'was dusty, old. But written legibly,
    There were the letters – – – – E.

CONGRATULATIONS

The last time I was
in this city,
     as this person,
I was buying flowers for my wedding
in the market.
     Congratulations.
Seven years ago.

Today, I walk to the courthouse,
sign the certificate,
wait minutes that feel like hours.
Then the prothonotary
calls me by My name,
and like Mary in the garden
I raise my head
and find myself,
not among the dead
     but the living.
I buy myself perfume,
not to cover the stench of a decaying corpse
     but to commemorate the resurrection.
     See, my daughter was dead and is alive again.

In this body,
     through these eyes,
the city has never looked more lovely.
I want to hug everyone
     in their bodies,
ask them all their names

and tell them mine.
I used it for years,
but today it feels fresh on my tongue—
sweet like the syrup in the crisp cold coffee
I sip to celebrate.
At work, the news starts to circulate,
and they cautiously
poke their fingers in my hands
and my side
and say, *Congratulations...*
with a question mark.
I nod and smile,
amused by their confusion.
Because why should *congratulations* be reserved for
    weddings,
    and babies,
    and promotions?
Why not also for
    the retreat from labor,
    the laying to rest of a body
    held hostage by hospice,
or the reclamation of a name?

I am my beloved's, and she is mine.
Congratulations.

BUMBLING

I swore that I would never find a mate
By algorithm, app, or some such means.
But when it comes to finding men to date,
Statistically thence my best chance leans.
But photos grainy, doctored, and obscene
Do flood my options, clutter up the feed.
They say, "I seek myself a curvy queen."
Or lame lines like "Hey, girl. Let's grab a mead."
Despairing for myself, I hit "delete."
A fortnight later, swiping for a match.
"Can you send me a picture of your feet?"
These master baiters angle for a catch.
    So I continue bumbling, stumbling on.
    Maybe the next I spy will be "the One."

SEAFARERS

Lord, when I said I wanted something slow,
Love at a pace of which I could be sure,
I'd hoped at least the warmth of each would grow
At equal rates—not this one-sided lure.
So how long should I wait for it to take?
Another year—or more—spent on my own?
I'm tired of crying salt tears when I wake.
I'm tired of spending one more night alone.
Yet something tells me patience is the key.
No ship to jump. I'm standing on the sand.
Pick up the oars, turn my back to the sea.
They've never had a man drown far inland.
    They don't have the same fears I've faced before.
    Then he says, "Sigh no more"—both feet on shore.

SANCTIFIED SOFA

You were here four days ago,
but the couch is still anointed with
    your cologne.
Now home smells like you.
    Or maybe you smell like home.

COMMUNION

The thing I thought would terrify me most
Was yielding my corporeal form to you.
For last time I was treated like the Host
Spit out instead of swallowed in the pew.
My nourishment rejected out of hand
And mandate of "come, taste and see" refused.
Consid'ring me unsatiating, bland,
He chose to starve, and both of us abused.
Yet you returned for seconds and for thirds.
The easy part was laying out the feast,
But how much harder 'tis to share the words
Composing in the bosom of the priest.
    Too soon to share these vespers without art
    Or whisper sacred secrets of the heart.

MORNING COFFEE

The day begins with ritual sublime.
His fingers skim the porcelain, bless the mug
That will receive the beverage divine—
That scalding, soothing, caffeinated drug.
The water in the kettle starts to boil.
The grinding of the beans, as one assumes
Position languid. Later we will toil,
But now we savor flavor as it blooms.
The cream comes in. The spoon stirs it around.
First sip slides down, awakening the mind.
Lip-smacking "ah" is now the only sound.
Why break the day with language more refined?
    For why must talk this early be endured?
    No need for words till second cup is poured.

MOUSETRAP

The newly-coined term "trigger"
    Gets thrown around these days,
And some make it seem bigger
    Than it is in many ways.

The word evokes the image
    Of a gun held to your head,
Or of a once-loved visage
    That now fills your mind with dread.

Or perhaps you still tiptoe around
    Talk of when you faced your doom.
A flashing light or sudden sound
    Sends you running from a room.

But what about for all of those
    Who were never close to dying?
For those who neither fought nor froze,
    But instead coped by complying?

No one talks about the little stuff
    As you go about your day
That reminds you of being "not enough"
    And "too much" anyway.

It's a song played on the radio,
    Or an apple in the store,
The color of those eyes that haven't
    Seen your skin before.

It's the way a forehead scrunches,
     Or restless legs that jigger.
The way a kneecap crunches—
     That's what I mean by "trigger."

Those tiny, microscopic things
     That send you rushing back,
Like mousetraps with tight-coiled springs,
     Primed and ready for attack.

Only, there's thousands on the floor,
     And someone turned out the light.
And they said, "Go and find the door,"
     With no safe path in sight.

But would running from that savory cheese
     Really make it safe for you?
There's no more fawn or flight or freeze.
     There's no way out but through.

HOPEFULLY

To say I'm hopefully in love with you
Does not in any way a doubt connote.
It doesn't mean someday it will be true,
Or that for now I do but only dote.
It means that I've abandoned childish things,
Like unrequited love and men who make
A fool of me, desiring naught but flings.
My over-trusting heart must for its sake
Give up on being hopelessly in love.
For I was taught that true love always holds.
The action, not the word, is what will prove—
No matter what uncertainty unfolds.
    In all ways love protects and perseveres
    And hopes to spite my antiquated fears.

IN THE STARS

Second star to the right and straight on till morning
sounded so much simpler when I was young.
Now, diving into the esoteric evening sky
spread out
like a
patient etherized upon a table,
I begin to see what they mean
when they talk about how
    small
    smol
    so tiny
we are and
how the stars outnumber
the grains of sand on
all the beaches of
the earth.

I'm reminded of the time in ninth grade when
we dissected fetal pigs.
Pulling the skin away,
fascia folding back
oh so slowly—
then all at once the jaws crack,
    maw wide—
    slit the belly,
    spill the guts.
The ugly truth out there for all to see,
the beauty in the intricacy
of vessels and veins

and nerves and kneecaps.

I look up into the sky and it all starts to peel back—
layer by excruciating layer—
revealing things I don't
    want to know,
    need to know,
    have always known
about myself.
All of it is me, every star and orb and constellation
stillborn, forever forgetting to breathe.

The smell of formaldehyde chokes my throat,
turns my stomach.
    Why don't you go get a drink,
    my Teacher says.
It's not a suggestion.
I step out into the hallway
and drink from a firehose,
gasp, drink some more.
Now I'm swimming in a sea of stars,
and I don't know which way is up or
    down.
Depth has never scared me—
only not being able to reach the bottom,
kick off,
resurface.
Yet the still smol Voice says,
    Drown.

I close my eyes and sink.
Salt scours my nose—
    all chemical confusion cleared away.
My skin wrinkles—
    it was always this thin.
Crushing pressure pops my lungs—
    turns out I never needed them to breathe.

I have died and been reborn
    a thousand-thousand times.
Not stillborn at all,
just ever-hovering
between Birth and Death,
wrapped lovingly in the waters of the Womb and Sky.

SATURN'S RETURN

When I was little
I thought I wanted to be an interior designer,
    renovating, reforming,
    making all things new.
Then it was a teacher,
    showing people how to
    be more human.
Then a seamstress,
    stitching a broken world
    back together.
Then a mother,
    rocking a child to sleep, or
    picking flowers in the garden.

And it took me three decades to discover
what the guidance counselors never told me—
that I didn't have to choose,
    that I was never going to grow up,
        that I contain multitudes,
that what I do with my time
is ten times as important
as what's on my name tag.

But I think if I only ever get to do one thing
for the rest of my life,
I want it to be this—
    to connect with the Divine
    in a way that makes my soul feel
    like it is coming Home,

and to help the other people at
my fingertips
do the same.

If that happens in my hearth and home,
        immaculate.
If that happens through my pen,
            incandescent.
If that happens from a pulpit,
                inspired.
If that happens on my deathbed,
how fucking *holy, holy, holy.*
I will have been training my whole life,
and I will finally be ready.

CURE WOUNDS

I am a cleric, like my mother before me,
but this realization only came at thirty
when I decided to reclass myself.
Starting a new character sheet wasn't an option.

I look at the woman I've known
    for forever—
        level twenty, thirty-five years
        fighting dragons and
        navigating dungeons—
and I feel small again.

Never have I ever—
    will I ever—
        stick an IV,
        stitch a wound,
        start a beatless heart.
Little hands, too small to stanch the bleeding.

But I will always—
    will I ever—
        make you a cup of chamomile,
        hold your hand,
        dry your eyes.
Because don't we all start small?

Level one, Little One,
running to her mother with another
    scraped knee.

Spray the lidocaine,
give the kiss,
apply the band-aid.

Now for other little knees I do the same,
    like she taught me.
And anytime the boo-boo feels too big,
    like it will never—ever—heal,
I remember her words,
    One day at a time.
Level one, Little One,
    One level at a time.

IN THE BEGINNING

Grandma had a jewelry box,
    Small and wood and fine
Where she kept all the baubles
    That someday I'd call mine.
There were lacey chains of gold,
And costume pieces bold,
And family heirlooms old
    That still possessed their shine.

When she went to the nursing home,
    The task fell to my mother
To sort through everything inside—
    No job for either brother.
She took the whole collection
Home with her for inspection,
And began to make election—
    If keep or sell she'd rather.

She called me in to help her,
    And I could scarce say no.
When would I have another chance
    To my ancestors know?
For in the glittering lot,
We found what time forgot—
Several gold bands bought
    For hands joined a century ago.

Held together by a pin,
    A half dozen wedding rings.

A brilliant one with purple stone
    Pulled at my own heartstrings.
But such precious family lore
Would be recounted nevermore,
Thanks to the stroke that bore
    Away those memories on its wings.

I kept the ring of amethyst
    With its white gold filigree.
My mother kept the wedding rings,
    To guard her ancestry.
But at the bottom of the pile
We found what took a while
To puzzle out. A small textile
    Circle stitched—a holy mystery.

No bigger than a nickel
    Was the little leather token.
A silken ribbon frayed by time,
    Once held the talisman bespoken.
Something bulged inside
The tiny yellowed hide.
No way I could have pried
    Or without damage opened.

Screwing up my courage,
    I grabbed a little pair of shears
And prepared to cut what had
    Been undisturbed for years.
Inside the pendant round
By blanket stitches bound,

A bit of wool I found
    And a writ that stirred my fears.

The scritta paper stored inside
    Had a verse of Latin print.
The type was so imposs'bly small
    That to read it one must squint.
I dreaded what released
Demon, poltergeist, or beast,
Once contained by a priest,
    I'd freed with this bit of lint.

So to the internet I turned
    To translate the puzzling script,
Terrified that I'd unleashed
    Something creepy from its crypt.
My fears quickly retreated
Once I had a chance to read it
In English. I proceeded
    Now with new knowledge equipped.

I found with more investigation
    A scapular, the thing was called,
And often they were with some verse
    Or word from God installed.
And what word had been selected
For this token I'd dissected?
THE Word resurrected,
    And that old tale recalled.

"In the beginning," it begins.
    That chapter I know well.
Pure poetry it is to me,
    Reverberating in each cell.
Memorized when young,
Those words have always sung
A sentiment my tongue
    Could not in its mean language tell.

When John wrote "The Word made flesh,"
    He pronounced all flesh was good.
Light shines out through every pore—
    Innate sin is a falsehood.
For how could Holy God
Dwell in a broken bod,
If it was so flawed
    As to have in damnation stood?

But there's beauty in the brokenness—
    There has been from the start.
There's no such thing as "God-shaped holes"
    To fill inside your heart.
For if God the Man—
In the works since time began—
Was always the plan,
    We two have never been apart.

Every bit of God's creation
    Is infused with the Divine.
The Catholic mass embodies this
    With simple bread and wine.

And yet for centuries
The popes all censured these
Crude carnal theologies,
    Causing dissenters to repine.

There were Catholics in my family tree,
    And some Lutherans, now deceased.
To whom had this token belonged?
    And what were their beliefs?
For I read that John's epistle
Was left out of the Missal.
What I'd found in this vessel,
    Was reserved for just the priest.

A Lutheran of the laity
    Might have owned it, yes.
But what if by a Catholic
    It once had been possessed?
What if this tiny page
Hidden in its leather cage
Had once served to assuage
    One by Rome so dispossessed?

One for whom the mystery
    Of God enduring birth
Was denied—that key reminder
    Of their own flesh's worth.
So by the Word instead,
To supplement their bread,
Daily secretly was fed,
    Until they left this earth.

Now in my own fleshy hands,
    I hold this tiny wonder.
And the guilt creeps in for having
    Cut the thing asunder.
Perhaps I was too bold
To ransack the fragile, old
Scapular made to hold
    Gospel from this Son of Thunder.

"But isn't that the point," I ask,
    "that one thing first must die
Before another can be born?"
    Therein does the mystery lie.
All acts of regeneration
Begin with incarnation,
And our own salvation
    Is in change, not stagnancy.

I'm thankful for the wisdom
    That space and time transcend—
This reminder from my ancestor,
    Whom to God I now commend.
We mustn't fear destruction
Needed for reconstruction.
And the sum of this instruction:
    "In my beginning is my end."